THE WINGMAN

A Reflection

the WINGMAN

leaving everlasting
love, legacy & lessons learned

Jon Anfinson

The WINGMAN by Jon Anfinson

R HOUSE PUBLISHING LLC FIRST EDITION, May 2024

Copyright © 2024 BY AMY ANFINSON

ALL RIGHTS RESERVED. No portion of this book may be reproduced, stored, in a retrieval system, or transmitted in any form or by any means-electronic, mechanical, photocopy, recording, scanning, or other except for brief quotations in critical reviews or articles, without prior written permission of the publisher.

PUBLISHED IN THE UNITED STATES BY R HOUSE PUBLISHING LLC, DALLAS, TEXAS

R House publishing titles may be purchased in bulk for educational, business, fundraising, or sales promotional use. For information, contact R HOUSE PUBLISHING - JC@rhousepublishing.co

ISBN-13: 9780997692334

WWW.RHOUSEPUBLISHING.CO

R HOUSE PUBLISHING LLC

DALLAS, TEXAS

Cover Interior Design by Emma Elzinga, Inksplatter Design

10 9 8 7 6 5 4 3 2 1

To Amy
the love of my life

CONTENTS

Forward IX
Part One: The Wing Man Answers 1
    Amy and Jon Dialogue 3
Part Two: Insight & Guidance from The Wing Man . . . 19
    Section 1: Navigating Life's Ups and Downs 21
    Section 2: Embracing The Journey 23
    Section 3: The Legacy We Leave: Lessons from Mom 25
    Section 4: Faith Through the Pause 27
    Section 5: Promises: A New Approach to Success 29
    Section 6: The Genius In You 32
    Section 7: A Death Sentence VS. A Destiny Sentence 36
    Section 8: All About Divorce 38
    Section 9: Let's Talk About Suicide 41
    Section 10: It's The Small Things That Count 43
    Section 11: Soften Your Story 45
    Section 12: Attitude - The Architect of Your Destiny . 48
    Section 13: Navigating the Fast-Paced World 54
    Section 14: Harnessing Desire: A Pathway to Success for Teens . 59
    Section 15: Legacy and Lessons: Jon's Reflections 67
Conclusion by Jon Anfinson 71
Afterward by Amy Anfinson 73
Acknowledgement 75
Connect 77

FORWARD

Dear Loved Ones,

As I sit down to pen these words, I am acutely aware of the fragility of life and the preciousness of each passing moment. My journey with terminal brain cancer has taught me more than I could have ever imagined. It has also driven my faith into deeper gear, and when Amy, my wife, suggested I answer a few questions from family and dear friends, I was inspired to write this as I feel compelled to share some reflections with you all.

First, to the young adults reading this, I urge you to embrace every moment of your life with passion and purpose. I spent most of my lifetime serving youth. Although I imagined my coaching business to continue much longer than it will, I can see now that it still will through those I have already reached and the many who will read this after I am gone. Recognize that it's easy to get caught up in the hustle and bustle of daily life, but remember to pause, breathe, and appreciate the beauty that surrounds you. You are growing up in a different time than me, but nothing is wrong about that. You are equipped to be fully who you are, and that you must. There are simple things to keep in mind: learn to love yourself, and it will be easy to love others and attract the right people to love you. Learn to trust yourself, and God will continue to entrust you with everything that is meant for you. And take it from a dying man or for the love of God - Take risks, follow your dreams, and don't let fear hold you back. Life is too short to play it safe. If you need support or direction, stay connected to Amy; she can help shine a light on your path.

To the older generations, I implore you to cherish the relationships that truly matter. In the end, it's not the wealth or possessions we accumulate that define us, but the love we give and receive. Take the time to nurture your connections with family and friends, for these bonds will sustain you through the darkest times.

Love deeply and purely, without reservation or hesitation. Be present, always. Trust the universe's flow and know there is so much good to align with. Hang on loosely: Let go of grudges and grievances (against self and others) and instead choose forgiveness and compassion. Life is too short to hold on to anger, resentment, or blame. Make amends, mend broken fences, and savor the joy that comes from authentic human connection. And dream! Come on! Don't use age as an excuse. Whatever you have been contemplating – do it. You're more ready than you realize.

As you journey through life, remember to hold on to the memories that bring you joy and comfort. These moments, big and small, are the threads that weave the tapestry of your life. Take photographs, write letters, and create lasting mementos you can treasure forever. And when the time comes to say goodbye, know that these memories will live on in the hearts of those you leave behind.

In closing, I want to express my gratitude for the love and support you have shown me throughout my journey and throughout the course of my life. Though my time may be limited, I know I am at peace, surrounded by love, and grateful for every precious moment I have been given. May you live a life that you love. My wish has not wavered in this life of mine… My dream for you is that all your dreams come true.

Your Wingman-
With everlasting love,
Jon

Part One

THE WING MAN ANSWERS

A note from Amy Anfinson:
    I'd like to share how this book came about and also why it was created in two parts.

    After weeks of what we thought was a severe sinus infection that led to extreme headaches and fatigue, on August 16th, we received Jon's diagnosis. Since we are not strangers to trusting in divine timing, we were not surprised that all of our close friends met us at the emergency room while finding out about this terminal diagnosis. We cried, prayed and even found joy amongst the love we all had for each other. The surgery was scheduled for the following day, August 17th and we were relieved to have clarity about what was causing his headaches and for the first surgery to go smoothly.

    The first procedure was to relieve pressure. The surgeon explained that if Jon had waited to be seen in just two weeks, he wouldn't be walking, and in four weeks, he would be gone. Four days after the first surgery, he had a follow-up surgery to remove as much of the tumor as they could in order to "give him some more time." We all braced ourselves for the second surgery as Jon was extremely weak. But we were surprised when he awoke blissfully and happy. He exclaimed to me, "I just wanted to see your face again." He shared, "I went somewhere."

I asked, "Where did you go?"

He answered, "I went to battle and I won. There was an army of angels around me."

Based on his peaceful disposition and his eagerness for what was to come, he most certainly had an army of angels around him. I documented and recorded most of the synchronicities and will share them in the near future.

Over the months, many friends and family reached out and asked to talk with him. This delighted Jon and he embraced every single invitation to share a part of himself with others. One friend, Judy Cochrane (author, ghostwriter, and publisher), naturally suggested I ask him questions and *document* his answers. At the same time, another friend, LoriAnn Garner, asked if she could spend Zoom time with him, where she would interview him in podcast style while they discussed his passion for life and people, especially highlighting the youth he served and why he chose to serve them. Below, you will see these come together in a Part One and Part Two where we have a series of questions and Jon's answers and the interviews to follow.

Watching him move through this with his innate peace and kindness has been remarkable. The friends I mentioned above were right to follow their intuition and trust that we would someday all have something precious and profound in our hands.

Although Jon was not able to hold this in his hands, it is in his wings now. I am elated to share that before he transitioned, I was able to surprise him by telling him he would be a published author. He was thrilled to share his wisdom and his heart.

He was indeed my wingman, but 100% welcomed becoming a wingman to all who would hold it in their hands.

NOTE: Thank you to all who contributed to this book. We embraced and appreciated all of your questions, especially your hearts.*

Some questions were condensed and may be unrecognizable by the questioner.

AMY & JON DIALOGUE

AMY: All right, let's begin. Would you consider life a place to learn or a playground? And why?

JON: Well, it's kind of a combination answer; Yes. I look at it as a place to learn. But how you learn is to use life as a playground.

AMY: I like that.

JON: First, if you take learning too seriously, I don't think you learn. You've got to *enjoy* the learning process. You need to have fun going through the learning process. And you need to laugh at the learning process. I mean, so yeah, it has to be a playground first.

AMY: Love it.

AMY: All right. Question number two: Is doing a good job that makes you good money more important than a lower-paying job that makes you happy?

JON: My answer is a lower-paying job that makes you happy. Suppose you don't like what you're doing but are making good money. You're not going to enjoy it, and you likely won't stay anyway.

AMY: What memories are the most important part of making an experience?

JON: Fun ones. You must enjoy doing what you're doing in business and life. If you don't enjoy doing what you're doing, you won't do it long. And if you don't do something very long, you're not going to create memories that are going to be happy. So, doing something you enjoy for an extended period of time is what creates happy memories for you.

AMY: The next question is: What is the best way to look at and handle any regrets that may happen in your life?

JON: Don't regret anything that happened.

AMY: How do you do that?

JON: Trust that whatever unfolded needed to. You have the opportunity to learn and grow from anything in life. And again, if it's work-related…choose things you enjoy doing so you don't leave room for regret or feelings of time wasted.

AMY: What do you do to move out of regret?

JON: Understand that perspective is everything. If you look at everything you do as a learning experience or as a teaching experience and enjoy/appreciate doing it in the first place, then you can't have any regrets. And if you can recognize it, you can create a shift in perspective.

AMY: Yes. Excellent. All right. What are two things you would advise a woman to do if they were single and 62 years old and hopes to someday find love again?

JON: Don't put a face to who you're looking for. Stay open to who it might be. You never know. Find someone who treats you like a best friend..someone who wants to laugh with you and have fun. And understand that 62 is still young.

AMY: What is your favorite verse in the Bible and why?

JON: My favorite verse of the Bible is Isaiah 40:31. "But those who wait on the Lord shall renew their strength. They shall mount up with wings like eagles, they shall run and not be weary, they shall walk and not faint." (Isaiah 40:31 NKJV).

AMY: Yes, that's a great one. And that has always been your favorite… And why is that your favorite one?

JON: Well, first off, it references eagles, and I love eagles: the bird and the band. And secondly, it references walking with God and understanding that you can do *anything* with God.

AMY: What is the best advice you received on how to navigate life?

JON: Understanding that everything is happening for us, not against us.

If we look at everything in the right perspective, everything happens for us. It's a matter of seeing the silver lining in everything that happens and understanding that no matter what you're going through, there is a positive end result. You just have to open your mind and your heart to see what that really is.

AMY: Describe your most perfect day.

JON: My most perfect day, I would say, is enjoying time at the lake with my wife and friends. Taking the boat out early in the morning when the water is calm and soaking up all of God's beauty. Maybe go to a nice restaurant for dinner or stay in and grill. Then, enjoy watching the sunset, hanging with friends, chatting and laughing…then planning our next shenanigans.

AMY: This question is about your mentoring experiences. Can you share a story about a time you mentored someone and saw a positive change in their life? And how did that make you feel?

JON: I was actually mentoring a manager when I was in the hotel business. I mentored him to work toward a promotion as an area district manager, and he was the right kind of guy for it. He just really was.

AMY: And the second part of the question is how that made you feel?

JON: How did that make me feel? It made me feel great because I realized I was helping him fulfill a dream that he had always wanted. And I've always realized that when you help someone get a goal or a dream and end up accomplishing it just to see their face light up - is really, really cool and ultimately the most satisfying experience one can have. (sigh) Yeah.

AMY: This question is about life lessons. Looking back, what key life lessons have you learned that you'd like to pass on to others?

JON: Life Lesson number one: Don't be afraid. Do it.

Take the chance. Bet on yourself. You don't want to end up in the end and regret not trying because chances are you're gonna realize you could have done it, and I don't want anybody to regret not doing something that they could have done.

JON: The second life lesson would be not letting the music die in you. In other words, if you've got an idea, do something with it. You know, like writing a book, composing a song, etc. And don't be afraid to reach out and help someone because you're afraid of what they'll think about you. Chances are, if you help someone, they're going to appreciate you more than you'll ever know. So when you get the chance to reach out and help someone do it.

JON: Third life lesson: I have always tried to do everything I have done in my life, my business life, my personal life, whatever, with as much integrity as I can. I want people to trust that when I tell them I'll take care of something, they don't have to worry about it anymore. I'll take care of it. To me, that's integrity. Following through with what you said you'll do and I think if more people used integrity in their lives, we'd have a heck of a lot better world.

AMY: This question is about family memories. What are some of your favorite memories with your children and stepchildren?

JON: Going on a family trip to an Airbnb with a huge pool and access to that serious grill setup. We spent the whole afternoon in the pool and the whole evening cooking fish and sitting in the big huge Lanai in the house. We sat around a big huge dinner table and scarfed down all the fish we cooked. It was a seafood feast. Wasn't it?

AMY: Yes, it was

AMY: How about with your kids?

JON: My favorite memory of doing something with my kids was going to a big lake in central Iowa. We used to go up there and just hang out at the beach. At the clubhouse, there was a big shelter house up there. We used to spend the entire day up there at the lake, and you know, we had water toys that we played with, and we'd play catch with balls and all that kind of stuff. So, the best memories were just spending the whole day at the lake having fun with my kids.

AMY: You also went on vacation to Disney World with the grandkids and Cody, which was a lot of fun. You've spent a lot of time with Drew. We went swimming with the sharks at Wonders of Wildlife now, and you had a lot of bonding time when you and Drew worked together on the house. And a lot of good memories.

Yes. Yes. (smile)

AMY: All right. Here's a question about personal achievements. What personal achievement are you most proud of and why?

JON: My most prized personal achievement was becoming a dad to my own and to your two great kids. I have two great stepkids, which I don't actually consider stepkids.

AMY: You helped raise them.

JON: (nod) The way I feel is that I have three sons. And one daughter.

AMY: You were amazing to them all. You helped raise my two. They were very young; you were a huge part of their life and treated them like your own. Thank you for that. Jon (bows head and holds hand in prayer position over chest)

JON: Is anyone a step? I don't even like the word. That's how I want them to feel. I want them to feel like they were actually my own kids, not stepchildren.

AMY: I think they do. You did that.

AMY: Name some influential people who were the most influential in your life, and how did they impact you?

JON: My grandpa taught me a lot about everything. You know, I learned electrical and plumbing work. I learned how to frame a house and how to take care of yards. When we had church camp, I learned how to paint and trim and learned about life. Grandpa taught me everything one could ever imagine about taking care of a piece of property, including taking responsibility in life.

JON: He taught me how to treat women, too.

AMY: Yes, he did.

JON: And how to treat people. He was a good man.

JON: Another one was Mr. Lincoln, who was the very first boss I had when I was working full-time for the Des Moines Golf and Country Club. Mr. Lincoln taught me how to treat people because he was the first black man I ever worked for. And I never once felt like I had anything racial. And he didn't look at me differently either. Yeah, we saw past colors. We just saw people for who they were exactly.

AMY: Here's a question about hopes for the future. What hopes or dreams do you have for your children's and stepchildren's future?

JON: It's a good question. My hopes and dreams for my kids are to help them find and fulfill their hopes and dreams. I've lived a pretty blessed life. I've got a lot of things accomplished. I've traveled the world. I've done all kinds of stuff. So, I've lived a pretty full life. So, my hopes and dreams now are to help them live a fulfilled, unlimited life.

AMY: How would you like to be remembered by your friends and family?

JON: That I was a yes man.

AMY: That's how I remember you. You got me to do more things in our 17 years than anyone else.

JON: Yeah. I want to help people fulfill their wishes, and they can't fulfill their wishes by saying no.

AMY: Here's a question about life's surprises. What event or experience in your life took you by surprise? That taught you something valuable.

JON: Oh, my brain cancer.

AMY: What did it teach you?

JON: It definitely took me *totally* by surprise. But it taught me to never take anything for granted. And then it also taught me to never forget that something can't be bigger. Because going through this whole journey, my faith has gotten bigger than I could have ever imagined. And I would have never guessed that could have happened.

AMY: Let's talk joyful moments. What are some of the simplest things in life that have brought you the most joy?

JON: I think the simplest thing that has brought me the most joy in my life has been going on walks with you because we always have such transformative conversations, questions, and discussions, and we always start them with appreciation.

AMY: Beautiful, yes, they were.

AMY: Allee (Evan's girlfriend) said Jon, you've always made a point to make me feel like part of the family. But I'll never forget our first family vacation together and our being responsible for the big seafood boil night at our VRBO. Wasn't that a fun adventure? And pretty tasty, if I say so myself. We've bonded a lot over experiences in the service industry and good eats in general. I want to hear about the favorite meal you've created and what led to it. Was it a vacation or a celebratory dinner? Or was it a meal you made one night after getting off of work? Whatever it is, I can't wait to hear about it.

JON: I gotta go with the one she brought up. That seafood boil we put together at that VRBO was off the charts. I think we had six or seven different kinds of fish, a couple of varying shrimp, some mussels, and some clams from the Fresh Market.

AMY: Oh yeah. All from a fresh seafood market right on the coastline.

JON: So yeah, that was definitely the top of the chart for me, and being able to share that evening with all the kids was just the icing on the cake. I wouldn't have enjoyed that meal better with anybody else but them. It was pretty magical.

AMY: It was. It was very special.

AMY: Alright, Question. What was one of the best college football game memories, and what made it so magical?

JON: Oh my, my most magical moment in college football was probably the first time I stepped out on the field at Iowa State. I grew up in a very small town. The most people we had in the grandstands was probably 350. In the first game that I got out on the field at Iowa State, there were 68,000 people in the stands and to hear the roar of the crowd, but more importantly to, come down the sidelines. And see all the people in the stands, leaning over one to give you a high five as you ran by and seeing their faces and the smiles on their faces and the lights in their eyes and to realize they were there to see us they were there to see me, and they wanted to reach out to me. I didn't realize I've talked about being impactful and that's being impactful. You are doing something to help them have a great time and feel fulfilled about being there. So yeah, the very first time I ever felt that enormity. It was so loud and crazy. Yeah.

AMY: What inspired you to start playing music?

JON: I think what inspired me the most was what I listened to. The first band that I ever followed that much was the Eagles, and I enjoyed their instrumentals. But I also enjoyed their harmony vocals. And I thought, wow, that harmony is so cool. I'd love to be able to do that someday.

AMY: Well, you do have the most amazing harmony voice.

JON: Thank you.

AMY: You asked, and it was given to you.

AMY: The next question is: what song reminds you of the moment you knew you were in love with me?

JON: Lionel Richie's, Lady.

AMY: The same person who asked that question commented that one of her favorite moments was hanging with Jon on Zoom and hearing you use the term "little lady." "All right, little lady."

AMY: The question is: How and where did the two of you meet, and what was the reason for relocating to Springfield?

JON: Well, we met at church in Springfield. I relocated to Springfield because of work. I was running hotels. I ended up picking up hotels in the Springfield area.

AMY: You also came back because your dad had cancer, and you were there for him, too.

JON: That's right.

AMY: Here's a comment and a question, Jon; you are blessed with the superpower of brightening every room you enter. There's zero chance of having a bad day after hanging out with you. Thank you for your laugh, your light and your heart. What advice would you give us on making a choice to be positive

JON: Don't let the doubt creep in in the first place. Nip it in the bud.

Yeah, catch the doubt before it gets momentum. I always say - care about how you feel.

AMY: You are good at that.

AMY: What's your favorite music?

JON: Any music that moves your soul. Jazz music. I like other genres, but if I had a choice to just sit and listen to something for hours and hours and hours on end, it would be jazz because of the difference in the music and the difference in the instruments… when you tie that all together? Yeah, I would. I would say jazz.

AMY: Alright, this is just a comment. No questions, just a beautiful, heartfelt message. "When I see your posts and updates, words just leave me. I've been dumbfounded and so damn sad. The strength that both of you show gives me hope. I think that Jon Anfinson is one of the greatest men I have had the privilege to know. His smile and laugh can light up a city. So much love to both of you."

JON: So precious.

AMY: All right. Here's another comment. So much love to you both. Amy, watching you navigate Jon's illness is so beautiful and so different than anything I experienced when I was a hospice nurse. It's the way our society should be dealing with death and dying, in my opinion. We have these bodies, for only God knows how long our soul and spirit are eternal. Being close to you and watching you navigate your life presently has been inspiring. I'm here for you and Jon.

JON: *smile

AMY: here's a question: What are your top two pieces of advice to young people today?

JON: My top piece of advice to young people:

Don't let the old people stop you.

Don't let negative people stop you.

Don't let the opinions of others stop you or stop you from doing what you feel like you should be doing.

AMY: Those are good ones, honey.

AMY: All right. What's the best pork chop you've ever had?

JON: The Ranch in Texas - with Judy and Bill.

AMY: What is the best vacation you have ever had?

JON: Abraham-Hicks, cruise to the Canary Islands with you.

AMY: Yeah, that was amazing.

JON: That was off the charts.

AMY: You also sat in the hot seat with Abraham.

JON: Yeah.

AMY: What makes you laugh every time?

JON: Being with my grandchildren and playing with them.

AMY: What fills your heart up?

JON: Spending time with my wife. *smile

AMY: What do you know for sure?

JON: That I have so many more friends than I ever would have imagined and I've been so blessed to spend time with a lot of them. To do all kinds of great things, and lately, I've realized how influential I actually have been in my life.

AMY: Love that.

JON: Interesting. That was one of the first books I had ever read. Cover to Cover was a book by John Maxwell called Becoming a Person of Influence.

AMY: So you took it all in and mastered it?

JON: I think so.

AMY: Awesome.

AMY: Here is another comment: "I hope one thing you know for sure is that you touch our hearts like no other human on this earth. Your heart is always felt when we are with you. We feel your deep love and appreciation and feel the same for you. That may feel normal to you. But that is not the norm out there, Jon. You are rare. I love you guys."

JON: That's precious.

AMY: All right. You know what, dear? We got through all the questions that I have been able to collect from friends and family.

JON: That was awesome.

AMY: I have one for you.

AMY: Okay, good. We'll wrap it up.

JON: That was fun. It was enjoyable. It was also very enlightening. We got some great friends.

AMY: Yes, we do—a lot of them.

JON: Yes, we do. We are blessed.

AMY: Definitely blessed.

JON: Yes.

AMY: I love that you feel so blessed and feel the influence that you've had in people's lives. That's what I wanted with all this.

JON: Good, I like it when my stuff works.

...approximately eight months later, while Amy & Jon were feeling love, appreciation and calm, Amy asked:

AMY: What do you appreciate?

JON: I appreciate my ability to stay calm and comfortable.

AMY: What else do you appreciate?

JON: I appreciate my ability to be a part of a bigger plan.

AMY: What are you ready for next?

JON: Peace and verbalizing my conversations with Jesus.

Part Two

INSIGHT & GUIDANCE FROM THE WING MAN

As Amy mentioned above, shortly after Jon was diagnosed with glioblastoma, a dear friend, LoriAnn Garner, interviewed him about his passion for mentoring the youth in our world. They spent countless hours together. At the time, LoriAnn privately questioned why she felt such a pull to do this. Six months later, I, Judy Cochrane, felt a desire to pull together the list of questions you have seen in Part One. Once finished, I felt there was a Part Two, but I couldn't figure out what to write. I combed through transcriptions that his wife, Amy, had shared with me but intuitively knew there was something already made for Part Two. After sharing this with Amy, she immediately thought of all these interviews LoriAnn had compiled!

They have been categorized to make it easy for you to read. They are not in order of importance but in the order in which they came about. Here, you will find a series of insightful interviews, where you will have the privilege of diving into the depths of Jon's soul and uncovering pearls of wisdom that illuminate the path to a fulfilling and purpose-driven life…in his world and your own. Plus, you'll feel his sunny disposition and playfulness, another of his greatest gifts to the world.

On behalf of the Anfinsons, please feel free to share Jon's words with both young and old.

Since his passion is always to brilliantly and lovingly serve the youth, please consider sharing with church youth groups, orphanages, foster families, public and private schools, etc.

in joy,

Judy Cochrane

Section 1:
NAVIGATING LIFE'S UPS AND DOWNS

Good morning, good afternoon, good evening—whatever it is where you are, I hope it's fantastic. I'm Jon and I'm here to talk about something that hits close to home for many of us, especially our teens and young adults: brain power breakthroughs. Now, why am I talking about this, especially now? Well, let me share a bit of my journey with you.

This past year has been a whirlwind for me, a time of transformation that's brought me face-to-face with some pretty intense challenges. Not too long ago, I was diagnosed with a glioblastoma—a type of brain tumor that's as tough as they come. But here's the thing, despite the science and statistics, I've chosen to bring a whole lot to the table in terms of fighting this. And in doing so, I've realized something crucial about life, especially for our youth navigating this complex world.

Everything we experience, every challenge, every triumph, is just a moment in time. It's not forever, even though it might feel like it. It's all about how we choose to approach these moments that define our journey. For me, understanding this has been pivotal. It's allowed me to see each day, each challenge, not as an insurmountable obstacle but as an opportunity for growth, learning, and, yes, even happiness.

Now, how can our teens apply this mindset to their lives? It's simpler than you might think. First off, recognize that every tough situation you find yourself in is just a moment. It's not going to last forever. You have the power to decide how you want the next moment to look and feel. Do you want it to be positive? Then, set that intention and watch as your mindset begins to shift.

Communication is key. In today's world, it's easy to feel isolated, especially with the challenges the pandemic has thrown our way. But reaching out, interacting with friends, and engaging in your community can uplift you in ways you might not expect. And remember, it's not just about making yourself feel better. When you reach out to help or simply be with someone else, you're also giving them a moment of joy, of connection. That's powerful.

Finally, humor and service. Never underestimate the power of a good laugh or the fulfillment that comes from serving others. Both can transform your perspective, taking you from a place of self-focus to one of shared joy and purpose.

So, to our teens and young adults out there, remember: life is a series of moments, each with the potential to be whatever you choose to make it. Embrace the challenges, reach out for connection, find humor in the everyday, and always, always look for ways to serve those around you. This is how you navigate the ups and downs of life, turning each moment into an opportunity for growth and happiness.

No matter what you're facing, you're not alone. We're all in this together, navigating this crazy, beautiful journey called life, one moment at a time. Let's make each one count.

Section 2:
EMBRACING THE JOURNEY

Hey there, young men and women looking for those nuggets of wisdom on your path to success. I'm Jon, and I've been where you are, searching, striving, and sometimes stumbling on my way to finding what it means to truly live a successful life. It's not just about the highs; it's also about navigating the lows with grace and resilience.

I chatted with my friend Chaz not too long ago. He's an ordained pastor, grief counselor, and hospice practitioner. Talking to him always brings new insights, and this time was no different. Our conversation reminded me of the incredible journey life is and how important it is to share what we learn with each other, especially when it comes to dealing with tough times.

Now, I know what you might be thinking. "Jon, what do you know about my struggles?" Well, I've been through my fair share. For starters, I'm currently battling brain cancer. But I've also had the privilege of a pretty blessed life filled with success in business, a beautiful family, and the opportunity to work with some of the greatest minds out there, like John Maxwell and Zig Ziglar. Yet, it's not the accolades or successes that define us; it's how we handle the challenges that life throws our way.

You see, it's all about how you react to what life hands you. There's a quote by Victor Frankel that really hits home for me: "Between stimulus and response, there is a space. In that space is our power to choose our response, and in our response lies our growth and freedom." That's the crux of it. We can't control everything that happens to us, but we can control how we respond to it.

I want to say to the young men and women out there: use that space wisely. Choosing to react in a way that propels you forward helps you grow and maintains your freedom to choose your path in life. It's okay to pause and take a breath before deciding how to move forward. That's where your power lies.

In facing cancer, I made a conscious decision not to see it as a death sentence but as an opportunity to cherish every moment I've got. I want to spend my days sharing time with friends and family and with you, sharing my experiences in the hope that you can glean something valuable from them for your own journey.

Remember, it's not just about building a successful career or making money; it's about building a life that you can look back on with pride, knowing you made the most of every moment, good and bad. It's about staying true to yourself, leaning on your faith or whatever gives you strength, and always, always moving forward with intention.

So, to all of you young folks trying to make your mark in the world, keep pushing and keep striving, but also remember to pause and reflect on how you're responding to the challenges life throws your way. Your journey to success is about more than just reaching your goals; it's about how you grow, learn, and evolve along the way.

Let's make this journey together. Keep asking questions, keep seeking answers, and above all, keep choosing responses that lead to growth and freedom. That's how you truly succeed in life.

Section 3:
THE LEGACY WE LEAVE: LESSONS FROM MOM

Hey again, young folks! I want to share something a bit more personal this time, something that's close to my heart and has been a beacon of light on my journey. It's about my mom. Now, you might wonder, "What does Jon's mom have to do with my path to success?" Bear with me because there are pearls of wisdom in the stories of those who've paved the way before us.

My mom is an incredible force of nature. She moved from Iowa to Arizona a couple of years back when she was 81! You see, after years of battling the snow, one day, she just decided, "Enough is enough." It took her longer to clear the snow off her car than to run her errands. That day, she chose change. She chose to rewrite her story from enduring the cold to embracing the warmth.

Now, here's the thing. My mom's decision to move wasn't just about escaping the snow; it was about seizing control of her life, about deciding that it's never too late to change your circumstances. She taught me from a young age that life is a series of choices, and these choices define us.

So, when I look at my journey, especially now as I navigate through my cancer diagnosis, I draw strength from her resilience. She's taught me that it's not the circumstances we find ourselves in but how we choose to respond to them that matters.

Let's get real for a moment. Life's going to throw some heavy stuff your way - it's a given. But, remember, between what happens to you and your response lies a moment of choice. And in that moment, you have the power. You can choose to let your circumstances define you, or you can define your circumstances.

When I shared my diagnosis with my mom, her strength was unwavering. She said, "Jon, this is just another chapter. How you write it is up to you." And she's right. Every day, we get to write our story. And while I'm in this chapter, I'm choosing to fill the pages with moments that matter, with love, with lessons, and with laughter.

To you, the young men and women carving out your paths, I want to pass on this wisdom. Look to those who've gone before you. Draw from their strength, learn from their choices, and when the time comes, make your own decisions with courage and conviction.

In this journey of life, remember my mom's story. It's a testament that it's never too late to change your path, choose warmth over cold, and choose life. And as you move forward, remember that the most significant legacy you can leave is the impact you have on others, the way you navigate your challenges, and the choices you make along the way.

So, as we journey on, let's not just aim for success in the conventional sense. Let's strive for a life well-lived, full of choices that reflect our deepest truths, just like my mom did. In doing so, maybe we, too, can become beacons of light for those who follow.

Section 4:
FAITH THROUGH THE PAUSE

Hey there, young folks. Jon here. Today, I want to chat with you about something that's been a cornerstone of my journey, especially now as I navigate through the waters of a cancer diagnosis. I'm talking about faith. But not just any kind of faith—I'm talking about the kind you find in the quiet moments and the pauses of life.

You see, life's going to throw a lot at you. It's like driving on an interstate, fast and unpredictable. I remember hearing about a tragic accident recently—a dad and his kids gone in an instant. It hit me hard. It reminded me how precious each moment is and how suddenly it can all change.

I've been on this cancer journey for about five and a half months now. It's given me a lot of time to think a lot of pauses. And in those pauses, I've found my faith growing stronger. Faith, for me, isn't just about believing in something greater out there; it's about believing in the choices we make every day.

Viktor Frankel once said something that stuck with me: between what happens to us and our response, there's a space. In that space lies our power to choose, and that's where our growth and freedom come from. That space, my friends, is where faith lives.

Living in what my wife, Amy, and I call the 'faith frequency' means recognizing those moments of pause in your life. It's about taking a deep breath before responding to whatever life throws at you. It's in those moments you can really tap into your faith—faith in yourself, in your journey, and yes, in that higher power you believe in.

For all you young folks out there, I know it can feel like the world is on your shoulders. But remember, it's not just the big decisions that define you; it's also those small moments in between—the pauses. That's where you get to decide who you want to be and how you want to face the challenges ahead.

My faith has taught me to see each day as a gift, especially now. Every morning, I wake up, thankful for another day, and ask myself, "What am I going to do with this gift?" That's faith in action—choosing to see the good, make the most of my time, and help others do the same.

I encourage you to lean into those pauses in your life. Use them to reflect, grow, and connect with your faith. Whether it's faith in a higher power, in the universe, or in the good of humanity, it's your anchor. It's what keeps you grounded and gives you the strength to push forward, no matter what.

Choosing positivity over negativity, hope over despair, action over inaction—it all starts in those moments of pause. That's where you find the true strength of your faith. It's not about being overly religious or spiritual; it's about how you choose to live your life, the values you stand for, and the choices you make.

So, take those pauses. Breathe. Reflect. And let your faith guide you to make choices that lead to growth and freedom. Remember, how you respond to the challenges in life defines you more than the challenges themselves.

Keep pausing, keep reflecting, and keep choosing faith, my young friends. It's your most powerful tool on your journey to success and fulfillment.

Section 5:
PROMISES: A NEW APPROACH TO SUCCESS

Hey there, young folks. Jon Anfinson here. I've been thinking a lot about how we set ourselves up for success in life, especially around the new year when everyone's talking about resolutions and goals. Today, I want to dive into something that could really change the game for you: understanding the difference between resolutions, goals, and promises.

Let's start with New Year's resolutions. We've all heard it, right? The gym gets crowded every January, with people determined to lose weight or get fit. But what happens? Most of the time, by February or March, the crowd thins out. Why? Because resolutions often start with a burst of motivation that fizzles out quickly. They're like wishes we hope to stick to without putting in the real groundwork to make them a reality.

Now, let's talk about goals. Goals are important; they give us direction. But here's the catch: goals must be specific, achievable, and paired with a plan. Saying, "I'm going to the gym every day," is a start, but without a plan, it's just a statement floating in the air. Goals are about the long game, planning steps to get where you want to be, and adjusting along the way.

But there's something even more powerful than goals: promises. A promise is a commitment, not just to the task at hand but to yourself. It's about saying, "No matter what, I'm going to do this." When I promise myself something, it's not about the conditions being perfect; it's about doing it because I said I would. That's the kind of commitment that leads to real change.

Think about it: if you promise to do just ten pushups a day, that might not seem like much. But it's not the number that matters—it's the act of keeping that promise to yourself, day in and day out. And here's the beautiful thing about promises: they build trust within yourself. When you keep a promise, you're telling yourself, "I can rely on me." That builds confidence and self-esteem, which are crucial for success in any area of life.

So, what's more likely to stick? A resolution you make because it's that time of the year, a goal that's maybe a bit too vague, or a promise that you make to yourself, knowing that you'll do everything in your power to keep it? From my experience and what I've seen in others, the promises change us.

Here's another thing to consider: our brains are wired to respond to the commitment of a promise. When you make a real promise, your brain takes it seriously. You're more likely to follow through because breaking a promise feels much worse than not meeting a goal. It's about accountability—to yourself and, sometimes, to others.

This isn't just about personal commitments; it also applies to business and relationships. Promises have the power to transform not only how we work towards our ambitions but also how we interact with each other. They help us build trust and integrity, which are the foundations of any successful relationship or venture.

So, to all the young men and women out there setting out on your journeys to success, think about this: instead of making resolutions this year or even just setting goals, try making promises. Promise yourself about who you want to be, what you want to achieve, and how you'll get there.

Remember, success isn't just about reaching a destination.

It's about how you grow, learn, and evolve on the way there. It's about the promises you keep to yourself and to others that shape the path you take. So, make those promises, keep them, and watch how they transform your life.

Let's embark on this journey together, promising to be our best selves, step by step, day by day. That's how we build a successful life, not just in achievements but also in character and fulfillment. Take it from me; it's a journey worth embarking on.

Section 6:
THE GENIUS IN YOU

Jon's Dive into the Mind with Dr. Larry Farwell
Hey there, folks! I had the incredible opportunity to sit down with none other than Dr. Larry Farwell, a genuine mastermind in the field of neuroscience. This guy isn't just your average brain enthusiast; he's a Harvard-educated pioneer who's literally reshaping our grasp on what the human brain can do from inventing brain fingerprinting to discovering how the brain-computer interfaces, Dr. Farwell is leading the charge in unveiling the untapped potential nestled within our noggins.

His groundbreaking book, "The Science of Creating Miracles," isn't just a read; it's an invitation to revolutionize how we think about our minds. Blending neuroscience with the boundless possibilities of quantum physics, Dr. Farwell guides us through harnessing our brainpower to craft extraordinary lives. And let me tell you, this isn't just talk. This man walks the walk, consulting with top-tier leaders and global agencies, proving that understanding the brain can indeed change the world.

Now, let's dive into the gold mine, which is our brains. Chatting with Dr. Farwell opened my eyes to something monumental: our brains aren't just about processing and storing information. They're gateways to consciousness, to shaping the very fabric of our reality. It's astonishing to think that this organ, tucked away in our skulls, holds the key to manifesting the life we dream of.

Through my conversation with Dr. Farwell, a few key takeaways really stuck with me. First, we often underestimate the brain's capabilities, relegating it to tasks and memories.

But in reality, our brains are powerhouses of potential, capable of connecting us to a deeper consciousness and enabling us to manifest miracles in our lives. Yes, miracles! According to Dr. Farwell, tapping into our brain's full potential can lead us to a path of self-discovery and unimaginable achievements.

So, as we embark on this chapter, I invite you to join me in exploring how to leverage the incredible power of our brains. With Dr. Farwell's insights as our guide, let's challenge our perceived limits and inspire each other to create our own miracles. Buckle up; it's going to be an enlightening ride!

First off, Jon, let's talk about this amazing thing we all have – our brains.

Diving deeper into our conversation, Dr. Farwell illuminated some profound truths about our brains, fundamentally changing how I view not just my own mind but the collective potential of human consciousness. Here's what unfolded in our dialogue, with Dr. Farwell leading the way to a new frontier of understanding.

Harnessing the Brain's True Potential

Dr. Farwell shared, "The human brain is not just an organ for thought and memory; it's the seat of our consciousness and a bridge to creating realities beyond our regular comprehension." This was a lightbulb moment for me. We've all heard that we only use a fraction of our brain's capacity, but here was Dr. Farwell explaining just how vast the untapped territories of our mind are.

The Miracle of Consciousness

"The brain's fundamental role," Dr. Farwell continued, "is reflecting consciousness. Through it, we can expand our awareness and, believe it or not, influence the fabric of reality." This idea that our consciousness can shape our reality wasn't just philosophical musing. Dr. Farwell backed it up with neuroscience and quantum physics, bridging the gap between science and what many would call miracles.

Learning and Evolving with Our Brains

Our discussion then veered into how the brain learns and evolves. Dr. Farwell emphasized, "Every new experience, especially those that evoke strong emotional responses, offers a chance for the brain to rewire itself. This plasticity isn't just about adapting; it's a gateway to profound personal growth."

From Trigger to Transformation

One of the most impactful concepts Dr. Farwell introduced was using trigger moments for transformation. "When faced with challenges or negative stimuli, we have a choice," he advised. We can react in the moment, or we can use these experiences as catalysts to tune in to a deeper level of consciousness and reprogram our response." This approach to life's inevitable ups and downs offers a pathway to not just resilience but also self-evolution.

Quantum Reality and Creating Miracles

The most exhilarating part of our conversation was when Dr. Farwell dove into the quantum aspects of consciousness. "Our deepest desires and intentions can resonate at a quantum level, influencing the very events of our lives," he revealed. It sounded like something out of a science fiction novel, yet here was Dr. Farwell, explaining how this was not only possible but within our reach.

Living in the Faith Frequency

As we wrapped up, I reflected on how these insights from Dr. Farwell echoed through my own journey, especially amidst the challenges I've faced. We also discussed how "Living in the faith frequency," had become a mantra for Amy and I over the months. Everytime we felt fear or sadness, we found our way back to keeping the faith and lining up with that frequency and how that was key to our alignment. Dr. Farwell added, the faith frequency isn't about blind optimism. It's about aligning with a deeper truth of our potential and the universe's capacity to conspire in our favor when we tap into the right frequency of thought and emotion.

Joining Dr. Farwell in this discussion wasn't just enlightening; it was transformative. His teachings aren't just for the academically inclined or the spiritually curious. They are for anyone who dares to dream of a life beyond the ordinary, powered by the most extraordinary tool we possess—our brains.

As we continue this journey together, let's not just admire the brain for its complexity. Let's dive deep, harness its power, and maybe, just maybe, touch the edge of our own miracles.

Section 7:
A DEATH SENTENCE VS. A DESTINY SENTENCE

Hey everyone, Jon here. Today, I want to talk to you about something really important—facing the big stuff in life, like the end of it. Now, I know it might sound heavy, but stick with me, alright? I've been staring down my own mortality because of my health situation, and let me tell you, it's been a wild ride. But here's what I've learned and what I hope you can take away from it, too.

First off, nobody knows when their time's up. That's something I learned pretty quickly. At first, I thought, "Would I want to know if I could?" But then, I realized, nah, I want to live my life without a countdown. That's no way to enjoy the time you've got.

Now, about handling the idea of death—look, it's part of life. And how we face it says a lot about us. For me? I lean on my faith. It strengthens and reassures me that there's more to this story than just the here and now. And hey, I've decided, if I get a say in what comes next, I'm coming back as a pro golfer. Why not, right?

But here's the serious bit, the part I really want you to get—communication is key. I mean it. Talking about what scares you, what you hope for, and even what you want for those you leave behind makes this journey a lot less scary. My wife, Amy, and I talked about everything. And knowing we can share our feelings openly makes all the difference. We also recognized that my diagnosis was less of a death sentence as it was an opportunity for us to see that my whole life had divine synchronicity in it and a divine destiny that unfolded. So do you!

So, if you're ever facing something big, something that makes you think about the end, remember to talk about it. Find someone safe, someone who gets it, and just start the conversation. It's not about having all the answers; it's about not facing those questions alone.

And for anyone out there who might be struggling with the thought of not being here anymore, please reach out to others. Talk to someone. Heck, you can talk to me. Whether I am here in the physical or on the other side. There are people who want to help you navigate through those dark thoughts. There's an app called I Relate, designed just for this purpose. Don't go it alone.

To wrap this up, just remember to live your life fully, love deeply, and never be afraid to talk about the hard stuff. It's all part of this crazy journey we're on. And who knows? Maybe I'll see you on the golf course in the next life. Keep swinging, and keep talking.

Section 8:
ALL ABOUT DIVORCE

Hey there, Kiddo, it's Jon again. Today, I want to chat with you about something pretty personal and, for a lot of folks, pretty tough—divorce. Now, life's thrown its fair share of curveballs at me, not just with my health but in my family life, too. I've seen up close what divorce can do, not just to the couple but to their kids as well. So, let's dive into this, shall we?

Divorce shakes up your world, no doubt about it. But here's what I've learned through my own experiences and those around me: how we deal with these changes really counts. I've been both a dad and a stepdad, and I've seen how important it is to keep those lines of communication wide open, especially with the kids.

Kids, listen. If your parents are going through a divorce, it's okay to feel upset, confused, or even angry. These are all normal feelings. But here's the deal—talk about it. Find someone you trust, like a family member, a friend, or even a teacher, and just let it out. Keeping all those emotions bottled up doesn't do anyone any good.

And to the parents out there navigating through divorce, remember, your kids are watching and learning from you. How you handle this situation sets the tone. It's crucial to reassure them that they're loved, no matter what changes around them. And yes, it's complicated, and no, there aren't easy answers, but making sure your kids know they can talk to you about anything, that's golden.

Divorce doesn't mean the end of a family; sometimes, it's just the start of a new kind of family. It took me a while to understand that. As a stepdad, I realized families come in all shapes and sizes, and what matters most is the love and support you give each other.

Let's dive a bit deeper into family dynamics, especially during tough times like a divorce. It's personal, real, and something I've lived through. So, let me share a bit about my journey with my kids, both my own and my stepkids, during these transitions.

When you're a parent going through a divorce, each child reacts differently, and as a dad and stepdad, I've seen this play out firsthand. It's not just about splitting time or figuring out holidays; it's about maintaining that thread of connection, no matter what.

For my kids, I made sure to spend quality one-on-one time with each of them. This wasn't about grand gestures or expensive trips. Sometimes, it was as simple as grabbing a bite to eat, taking a walk, or just sitting down and talking about what was on their mind. The key was making each of them feel seen and heard during a time when everything around them was changing.

With my stepkids, building trust was crucial. Stepping into their lives, I wanted to be a stable figure they could rely on. So, I invested time in understanding their interests, like if one was into soccer, I'd make it a point to kick the ball around in the backyard or go to their games. For others who might have been into music or art, I'd show genuine interest in their hobbies and attend their concerts or exhibitions. It was all about showing up, physically and emotionally.

The biggest lesson here is that it's the small moments that count. A conversation over dinner, a shared joke, or a quiet moment together can mean the world. It's about building those bridges, piece by piece, until you've created a strong, new connection.

For those navigating through the complexities of blending families or dealing with the aftermath of a divorce, remember this: patience, persistence, and presence. Be patient with the process and with each other. Persist through the challenges because it's not always going to be easy. And most importantly, be present. In a world full of distractions, the greatest gift you can give your kids is your undivided attention.

So, to all the parents and stepparents out there, keep those lines of communication open, keep showing up, and keep building those bonds. It might take time, but it's worth every moment.

To sum it up, divorce is tough, but you're not alone. There's a whole world of people out there who understand what you're going through. Reach out, speak up, and never forget that even through the toughest times, there's a path forward together. Keep those conversations going, and remember, it's the love that makes a family, not just the titles or the traditional setups.

Alright, that's it for now. Keep your heads up and your hearts open. Talk soon

Section 9:
LET'S TALK ABOUT SUICIDE

Alright, let's tackle a really tough subject – suicide. It's heavy, but it's real, and sadly, it's something that touches too many lives. I've had personal experiences in my circle where this heartache has hit close to home, and I want to share some thoughts and resources that might just make a difference to someone out there.

First off, if you or someone you know is struggling, feeling lost, or just can't see a way out, I want you to know there's hope. There's always a sliver of light, even in the darkest places. Trust me, reaching out and talking to someone can feel like lifting a hundred-pound weight off your chest.

I've seen the pain and the what-ifs that linger after someone takes their own life. It's a wound that doesn't easily heal. But I've also seen the power of speaking up, of sharing those heavy thoughts with someone who cares. Sometimes, just knowing someone is there to listen, without judgment, can change the course of a person's day, maybe even their life.

So here's my advice: talk about it. If you're the one feeling down, reach out. And if you notice someone else struggling, be that person who reaches out to them. It doesn't have to be a deep, life-changing conversation. Just a simple "How are you really doing?" can open the door.

And let's not forget the hotlines and websites dedicated to providing support. These aren't just for crisis moments; they're there for anyone who needs to talk. The National Suicide Prevention Lifeline is a 24/7 service where you can speak to someone who gets it. They're at 1-800-273-TALK (1-800-273-8255). There's also a crisis text line – text HOME to 741741. It's free, it's confidential, and it could be the first step toward feeling better.

I want to wrap this up by saying life's tough, no doubt about it. But you, my friend, you're tougher. There's strength in seeking help and courage in continuing to fight another day. Keep those lines of communication open, lean on each other, and never underestimate the power of a listening ear.

Remember, your story isn't over yet; there's so much more to write. Stay strong, and let's keep this conversation going. Until next time, take care of yourself and each other.

Section 10:
IT'S THE SMALL THINGS THAT COUNT

Hey there, everyone! Let's dive into some real talk designed to help teens, young adults, and anyone else who finds value in what we've got to share. My goal? To help you thrive in this world, bring what you've got to the table, and create a life you're proud of and one that brings you joy and prosperity.

So, today, I want to focus on something simple yet profound—the idea that little things matter and knowing what to do isn't the same as doing it. This concept is crucial because it's those small, consistent actions over time that truly shape our lives. Imagine you've got a choice to take a simple positive action or, on the flip side, a simple negative one. These choices, repeated, determine the life you create.

I want to challenge you with this: would you be willing to pause for just 10 seconds before asking yourself, "Is this a positive step for me, or is it negative?" This brief moment of reflection can be a game-changer. It's about being impeccable with your word, even in a text message. Write it out, then pause. Reread it. Is it positive? If yes, send it off and brighten someone's day. If it's negative, tweak a few words. It's about making sure even the little interactions we have are filled with positivity.

Another thing I want to touch on is the importance of consistency and integrity. Doing the right thing, especially when no one's watching, speaks volumes about who you are. It's not just about others; it's about being true to yourself. When you look in the mirror each morning, don't hesitate to tell yourself, "I love you. You're doing great. Keep it up." It might feel odd at first, but trust me, it becomes a source of strength over time.

And remember, no success story is without its challenges. It's about not giving up, even when the road gets bumpy. Every small step, every consistent action, brings you closer to your goals. It's not about overnight success; it's about building a life of success, one small step at a time.

I want to leave you with this: life is a series of small decisions and actions. Choose positivity, choose consistency, and most importantly, choose to be true to yourself. And if you ever find yourself doubting or needing a bit of guidance, we're here. We are not just here to talk but to support you on your journey to success.

Until next time, keep taking those small steps, keep being impeccable with your word, and let's all strive to live a life filled with integrity. Take care, everyone!

Section 11:
SOFTEN YOUR STORY

Hey, young folks, Jon here, diving deep into a concept I'm super passionate about—*softening your story*. Now, you might wonder, "What's all this about?" Let me break it down for you in a way that hits home.

Imagine your life as a book you're writing every single day. Some chapters are filled with adventures, some with lessons, and some with a bit of heartache. But here's the kicker: how you tell your story, especially the challenging parts, can really shape how you see the world and yourself in it.

So, when I say "soften your story," I'm talking about looking at those not-so-great chapters and asking yourself, "How can I tell this story in a way that's kinder to me?" It's not about ignoring the hard stuff or pretending everything's all sunshine. It's about giving yourself some grace.

For instance, let's say you bombed a test you studied hard for. You could tell that story like, "I'm just not cut out for this." Or, you could soften it and say, "I gave it my all, and now I've got a better idea of how to tackle it next time." See the difference? The first way might make you want to give up, but the second way? It shows you're resilient and learning, which is what life's all about.

Now, you might think, "But Jon, is changing how I talk about stuff really going to make a difference?" Absolutely. Our brains are pretty incredible, and they pay attention to the stories we tell ourselves. By choosing words more about growth and less about blame, you're wiring your brain to see life as a series of opportunities, not setbacks.

This doesn't just help you. When you share your stories, soften them and create connections with others. You show them it's okay to be vulnerable and that we're all in this together, growing, stumbling, and getting back up again.

"Understanding the depth of our connections and the conflicts that arise within them requires us to consider our immediate reactions and the stories we tell ourselves," I often say. It's particularly true with those closest to us, where our emotional investments are highest. The challenge, as well as the solution, lies within our ability to pause. This moment of stillness is not about inaction but about creating space for clarity and understanding.

Communication is the key to nurturing relationships and resolving misunderstandings. "Listen actively and ask clarifying questions." This isn't just about exchanging words but about truly understanding the heart behind them. By repeating back what you think you've heard and sitting in the ensuing silence, you allow the other person and yourself to reflect on the true essence of the exchange.

I emphasize the significance of self-love as the foundation for all relationships. "Love yourself first". This inner love is your anchor, ensuring that when waves of conflict arise, you stand firm, not swayed by external turmoil.

Saying 'yes' more often than 'no' can open pathways to deeper connections and understanding. It's about embracing the possibilities of what could be rather than being held back by fear of what might go wrong. I suggest allowing yourself and those around you the space to explore, fail, and grow. This openness fosters an environment where genuine connections thrive, supported by mutual respect and understanding.

Remember, the journey toward stronger relationships and reduced conflict is paved with self-reflection, empathy, active listening, and love. I recommend applying the power of pause in every interaction. This conscious effort transforms potential conflicts into opportunities for growth and deeper understanding.

Embracing these principles enhances our relationships and contributes to a more compassionate world. Let's remember that each moment of misunderstanding is an opportunity. It's in these moments that we find the true strength of our bonds and our capacity for love and understanding.

So, take a moment next time you reflect on a challenge or share your story with a friend. Think about how you can soften the story to highlight your strength, growth, and the lessons learned. Remember, you're the author here. Write your story in a way that's true to you and shows how much you've grown.

And if you ever feel stuck, remember, I'm here rooting for you, sharing my own stories, and reminding you that every chapter, especially the tough ones, is a stepping stone to the amazing person you're becoming. Keep writing your story, my friends, with kindness, courage, and a whole lot of heart.

Section 12:
ATTITUDE – THE ARCHITECT OF YOUR DESTINY

Hello again. It's Jon, and today's topic is close to my heart and crucial for every teen and young adult out there: attitude. This isn't just about having a good or bad attitude; it's about understanding the profound impact your attitude has on your life's trajectory.

My journey has taught me that attitude begins with how you view yourself. The perspective you adopt towards yourself sets the tone for your entire day, your decisions, and ultimately, your life. I came across a book titled "Fish" by the owner of The Pike Place Fish Market, which beautifully encapsulates the essence of attitude in the workplace and, by extension, in life. It's about making the daily grind enjoyable, about choosing to bring a positive attitude into your surroundings, and watching how that transforms not only your day but the day of those around you.

This principle of bringing joy and a positive outlook to every situation has been a guiding light in my life, especially through the challenges I've faced. Whether in business or personal struggles, maintaining a positive attitude has opened doors, brought blessings, and established connections I could never have imagined. It's this attitude that people remember that draws them to support you in your time of need and ultimately shapes the world around you.

So, how can our teens and young adults cultivate this success-driven attitude? It starts with visualization and believing in the life you want to create. Create a vision board, digital or physical, and fill it with images of your goals and dreams. This visualization is a powerful tool; it serves as a daily reminder of what you're striving towards and keeps your attitude aligned with your aspirations.

Another simple but powerful tool is the use of affirmations. Whether through sticky notes around your room or digital notes on your phone, reminding yourself of your strengths and goals can significantly impact your attitude. These daily doses of positivity build up over time, shaping your mindset and, consequently, your reality.

Let me share a story that illustrates the power of attitude. A young man, against all odds, visualized himself in the VIP section of a football game. Despite his circumstances, he dressed the part and, with unwavering belief, made it into those VIP seats. This act wasn't just about watching the game from a better view; it was a declaration to the universe of his intentions. Today, he's a successful businessman who remembers where he came from and pays it forward by empowering others. His story is a testament to the fact that you can transform your dreams into reality with the right attitude.

Attitude is indeed everything. It's the foundation upon which you can build a life of success, joy, and fulfillment. To our teens and young adults: remember that your attitude is a choice. Choose positivity, choose to believe in yourself, and choose to see challenges as opportunities. These choices will architect your destiny.

And to everyone listening, know that you're not alone in navigating the complexities of life. We're here to support you, answer your questions, and help you cultivate an attitude that will open doors to endless possibilities. Let's make every moment count together.

Thank you for joining us on this journey. Remember, the power of a positive attitude can move mountains. Let's keep moving forward, one positive step at a time. See you in the next chapter of our adventure.

Harnessing the Power of the Four Agreements

In exploring the path to personal freedom and stronger relationships, especially for our youth, I often reflect on the profound simplicity of Don Miguel Ruiz's The Four Agreements. My wife Amy and I have integrated this book deeply into our work and personal lives. It offers a framework for navigating the external world and understanding our inner landscapes.

Be Impeccable with Your Word

The first agreement, "Be Impeccable with Your Word," is about the truth we speak to ourselves and to others. It's a call to honor our commitments and to speak with integrity. Remember, your word is not just what you say to others; it's also what you say to yourself. When you promise yourself something, honor it. This impeccability builds a foundation of trust within and around you.

Don't Take Anything Personally

The second agreement, "Don't Take Anything Personally," is pivotal, especially in our teen years when we're forming our identities. Understand that what others say and do is a projection of their own reality. When you truly grasp this, the actions and words of others won't shake your sense of self. This agreement teaches us resilience, helping us navigate the often tumultuous waters of adolescence and beyond.

Don't Make Assumptions

The third agreement, "Don't Make Assumptions," encourages us to seek clarity in our interactions. Misunderstandings, sadness, and drama can be mitigated simply by asking questions and expressing our true desires. This agreement empowers you to live with a sense of curiosity and openness rather than jumping to conclusions or living in a narrative built on unverified beliefs.

Always Do Your Best

Lastly, "Always Do Your Best" is about understanding that our best changes from moment to moment. It's a compassionate acknowledgment that while we aim for consistency in our efforts, our capacity varies due to external and internal factors. This agreement is a call to self-compassion and persistence, teaching us that as long as we do our best, we are on the path to personal growth and fulfillment.

These agreements are not just principles but tools for building stronger relationships and reducing conflict in our lives. They teach us to navigate our inner world with integrity, resilience, clarity, and compassion. As we apply these agreements, we create a life that is fulfilling and a true reflection of our highest selves.

Now, let me share my personal stories of how Don Miguel Ruiz's "The Four Agreements" has impacted my life. Integrating these principles into my life has been both a challenge and a profound journey of growth. My wife Amy and I have deeply explored these agreements, applying them in our work and personal lives. Here, I'll share some of the personal stories that illustrate the impact of living by these agreements.

INTEGRATING Be Impeccable with Your Word

Growing up and throughout my early business years, the importance of a handshake, a symbol of one's word, was paramount. This agreement resonates with me deeply because it represents a return to valuing integrity and commitment. A personal turning point came when I had to hold myself accountable for my promise, not to someone else but myself. It was a commitment to better health. The challenge was not in making the promise but in the daily effort to honor it. This journey taught me that being impeccable with my word starts with the promises I make to myself.

INTEGRATING Don't Take Anything Personally

One of the most challenging yet liberating experiences came from applying the second agreement in my interactions. I recall a moment when I received harsh criticism from a colleague. Initially, my gut reaction was defensive. However, remembering Don's guidance, I stepped back and realized this critique was more about the other person's insecurities and challenges than about me. This shift in perspective transformed a potentially conflict-ridden situation into one where I could offer support rather than defense. It was a profound lesson in the power of detachment from others' opinions and projections.

INTEGRATING Don't Make Assumptions

The third agreement, "Don't Make Assumptions," hit home during a misunderstanding with a close friend. Without direct communication, I had assumed their disappointment, which led to unnecessary tension. By finally having an open conversation, I realized my assumption was baseless. This experience underscored the importance of clear communication and the dangers of letting our assumptions dictate our relationships.

INTEGRATING Always Doing Your Best

The principle of always doing your best became particularly poignant during my journey through a significant health challenge. Facing physical therapy and the daunting path to recovery, I was confronted with two critical questions: Do I believe I can do this, and, more importantly, do I want to do this? This period of my life was a testament to the fact that "doing your best" varies from moment to moment. It taught me that my best under these circumstances was showing up for myself every day, no matter how small the progress seemed.

These personal stories are just snapshots of how "The Four Agreements" have shaped my path. They've taught me integrity, resilience, the importance of clear communication, and the power of perseverance. Each agreement, in its own way, has guided me to a deeper understanding of myself and my interactions with the world around me. It's a journey I continue to walk every day, learning and growing with each step.

As you embark on this journey, remember that mastering these agreements is a lifelong process. Each day presents new challenges and opportunities to apply these principles. The beauty of the Four Agreements lies in their simplicity and the profound transformation they can usher into our lives, relationships, and sense of self.

Section 13:
NAVIGATING THE FAST-PACED WORLD

Hello Folks, Let's discuss understanding and empowering Generation Z, focusing on their unique challenges and opportunities. As we navigate through their journey, it's crucial to understand the context in which they've grown up—a world markedly different from previous generations, shaped significantly by the digital age and the pandemic.

The Digital Native's Dilemma

Generation Z, the true digital natives, have had a distinct start to their careers, one that didn't involve stepping into an office or working alongside colleagues in person. Instead, their introduction to the working world was remote, shaped by screens and digital interfaces. This transition has implications for developing essential executive functioning skills such as critical thinking, mindfulness, being present, and learning boundaries with technology.

Fast Learning vs. Deep Learning

Thanks to the internet, this generation has mastered the art of fast learning. The pace at which they consume and learn information is unprecedented. However, this speed comes with its challenges. Essential skills that require time to nurture, often through personal interaction and face-to-face communication, are challenging to acquire in the fast-paced digital world. The question arises: Do these young adults see a need for these traditionally developed skills, or have they adapted to a new way of learning and interacting that suits their fast-paced culture?

The Value of Time and Personal Interaction

One of the most significant shifts for Gen Z is the transition from learning and interacting in a shared physical space to doing so virtually. This shift impacts how they learn and how they relate to others and build relationships. In a world where disconnecting is as easy as a click, the depth of personal interaction and the development of patience and understanding in communication can be lost. Yet, these skills enable us to connect on a deeper level, understand and be understood, and build relationships that withstand the test of time and challenge.

Seeking Balance in a Digital World

Considering the skills that Gen Z may need to thrive, it's not about discarding the incredible advantages and efficiencies that technology brings. Instead, it's about finding a balance. It's about recognizing that while technology can enhance our lives, it cannot replace the nuanced understanding, empathy, and connection from human interaction. Despite being more complex to measure and develop, these skills are crucial for personal growth, professional success, and societal cohesion.

Empowering Gen Z: A Call to Action

Empowering Generation Z means acknowledging the world they've grown up in while also emphasizing the value of skills developed through personal interaction. It involves creating opportunities for them to develop these skills in environments where they feel comfortable and supported. As parents, mentors, and educators, it's our responsibility to guide them, not by dictating what they should learn but by opening doors to experiences that enrich their understanding and abilities.

Understanding and Empowering Gen Z: Insights from Jon's Journey

In our rapidly evolving world, understanding the unique perspectives and challenges faced by Generation Z is crucial. As I've engaged with this vibrant generation, personally and professionally, I've gleaned insights essential for fostering communication and growth between generations. Here, I share my observations and the lessons I've learned in the hope of bridging gaps and encouraging mutual understanding.

Embracing Digital Natives

Gen Z, the first true digital natives, has a relationship with technology that is fundamentally different from any previous generation. Their fluency in digital communication and social media isn't just a phase; it's a profound part of their identity and worldview. Recognizing this, I've learned the importance of meeting them where they are—on platforms and in modes of communication where they feel most comfortable. It's not about discarding traditional methods but enriching our interactions with digital savvy.

Valuing Authenticity and Transparency

One of Gen Z's most striking traits is their deep appreciation for authenticity and transparency. This generation can spot insincerity and disingenuousness a mile away, which has taught me the significance of being genuine in every interaction. Whether it's in personal conversations, business dealings, or social media engagements, being true to oneself and honest with others is paramount. This authenticity fosters trust, a crucial foundation for any relationship.

Understanding Their Worldview

Gen Z has grown up in rapid change and considerable uncertainty. From economic recessions to climate change and social justice movements, these global events have shaped their perspectives and priorities. Engaging with them has opened my eyes to the diverse issues they care deeply about. By actively listening and seeking to understand their concerns, I've learned to better communicate with Gen Z and view the world through a broader, more inclusive lens.

Empowering Through Mentorship

My interactions with Gen Z have underscored the importance of mentorship. This generation is eager to learn, grow, and make an impact, but they also seek guidance and support from those who have walked the path before them. In my mentoring relationships, I've focused on empowering them to harness their unique strengths and navigate the challenges they face. It's not about dictating what they should do but rather about helping them discover their own path to success.

Celebrating Their Innovativeness

Finally, I am continually amazed by Gen Z's innovativeness and their ability to think outside the box. Their fresh perspectives and creative approaches to problem-solving have often led to breakthroughs in areas where others see barriers. We can foster an environment where innovation thrives by creating spaces that encourage creativity and genuinely valuing their input.

In conclusion, my journey with Gen Z has been one of learning, adaptation, and mutual respect. We can build stronger, more meaningful connections across generational divides by embracing their digital fluency, valuing authenticity, understanding their worldview, empowering them through mentorship, and celebrating their innovativeness. It's a journey that requires patience, openness, and a willingness to step into their shoes—a journey well worth taking.

Section 14
HARNESSING DESIRE: A PATHWAY TO SUCCESS FOR TEENS

Welcome to this special section on understanding and harnessing teens' desire for success, which is drawn directly from Jon's insights in his Brainpower Breakthroughs series. With his extensive experience in coaching and mentoring young adults, Jon illuminates the concept of desire, exploring its complexities and guiding young individuals and their parents through these pivotal years.

The Essence of Desire

Desire, in its simplest form, represents our wishes and wants, driving us towards things we believe will make us happy upon their fulfillment. Yet, when the source of a desire shifts from being self-driven to being influenced by others, it introduces a nuanced challenge for young adults. This chapter helps us understand this dynamic, offering guidance on approaching desires that originate from within versus those prompted by external expectations.

In discussing "The Essence of Desire," I want to help you understand the power and complexity of desires. Whether navigating your teenage years or entering adulthood, this conversation is for you. It's about distinguishing between the desires that spring from the core of who you are versus those shaped by the world around you. Let's delve into this together.

Embrace Your Internal Desires

Your desires are a compass. They're not just whims or fleeting thoughts; they're profound indicators of what makes you, you. When a desire wells up from within, it's authentic and deeply connected to your passions and dreams. These pursuits light a fire in your heart, compelling you to move forward, grow, and discover more about yourself.

I encourage you to listen to these internal whispers. They might guide you towards paths you hadn't considered, offering fulfillment and happiness that's genuinely yours. Remember, the journey to achieving these desires is as rewarding as the destination itself. It's a journey of growth, learning, and self-exploration.

Understand the Impact of External Desires

Now, let's talk about the desires that come from outside influences. These could stem from family expectations, societal norms, or the pressure to fit in with peers. While it's natural to be influenced by the world around you, it's crucial to recognize when a desire isn't truly your own.

Navigating these external pressures can be tricky. They might lead you to question your path or, worse, walk a path meant for someone else, leaving you feeling unfulfilled or lost. It's essential to differentiate between what you genuinely want and what others want for you. Ask yourself, "Is this desire truly mine, or am I pursuing it to meet someone else's expectations?"

Accountability, Responsibility, and Control

A significant part of pursuing desires, especially those influenced by others, involves grappling with accountability and responsibility.

It's understandable to feel apprehensive about the obligations that come with chasing a goal, particularly if that goal isn't something you're passionate about. This fear often stems from a perceived loss of control over your life and decisions.

However, I want to reassure you that feeling in control of your desires and, by extension, your life is about making conscious choices. It's okay to seek guidance and support, but remember; you have the power to decide which desires are worth pursuing. It's about balancing your autonomy with the world's inevitable influence.

Moving Forward with Your Desires

Reflecting on your internal and external desires is a powerful exercise. It's about understanding yourself better and making choices that align with your authentic self. Here are a few steps to help you navigate your desires effectively:

- **Self-Reflection:** Spend time with your thoughts. Understand what truly makes you happy and fulfilled. It's okay if this takes time or if the answers aren't apparent immediately.

- **Open Communication:** For parents reading along, engage in open, judgment-free conversations with your kids about their desires. Support their internal desires and guide them in navigating external influences without pressure.

- **Embrace Growth:** Every desire, whether fulfilled or not, is an opportunity for growth. Learn from every experience and use it to refine your understanding of what you truly want.

Remember that your desires are a reflection of who you are and who you aspire to be. Whether they're driven by internal passions or influenced by the world around you, understanding the essence of your desires is the first step towards a fulfilling life. Let's embark on this journey together with openness, curiosity, and the courage to follow our true desires.

Understanding Control and Accountability

In my journey of mentoring young adults through the "Transforming Your 20s" initiative, I stumbled upon a fascinating pattern that offers a wealth of learning for both young individuals and their guardians. The crux of this discovery lies in understanding the nuanced relationship between control, accountability, and the pursuit of desires. Let's unpack this together, shall we?

Grappling with Accountability and Responsibility

When we chase a desire, especially one that's deeply personal, we're stepping into a commitment. It's like signing an invisible contract that says, "I'm responsible for the outcomes of this pursuit." However, when this desire is influenced or presented by someone else, even with the best intentions, a sense of hesitancy creeps in. This hesitancy is about something other than the desire itself but the strings of accountability and responsibility attached to it.

Many young adults I've worked with expressed a subtle yet significant resistance to taking on desires that come with these "strings attached." This reaction isn't about laziness or a lack of ambition; it's a deep-seated need to stay in control of their lives and decisions. The thought process goes something like this: "If I pursue this desire, which isn't entirely my own, am I still in control of my path? Or am I conceding control to someone else's expectations?"

The Quest for Autonomy

The quest for autonomy is at the heart of this dilemma—a fundamental aspect of the young adult psyche. This age is all about exploring, making mistakes, learning, and, most importantly, asserting one's independence. The idea of being accountable to someone else's version of their desire feels like a direct threat to this autonomy. It suggests a path not fully chosen but somewhat imposed, which can be a hard pill to swallow.

Understanding this resistance is crucial for both young adults and those guiding them. It's not a battle of wills but a necessary phase of growth. The key lies in navigating these desires in a way that feels authentic and self-driven, even when they originate from external suggestions.

Embracing Desires on Your Terms

To young adults navigating this phase: Your feelings of wanting to maintain control over your life are valid and important. It's okay to question and critically evaluate the desires you pursue, ensuring they align with your true self. Here's how you can embrace desires on your terms, balancing accountability and your need for autonomy:

- **Self-Evaluation:** When presented with a desire, take a step back and ask yourself, "Is this something I genuinely want? How does it align with my values and aspirations?"
- **Setting Boundaries:** It's okay to set boundaries around pursuing these desires. Communicate clearly about what you're willing to take on and where you draw the line.

- **Taking Ownership:** Embrace the aspects of the desire that resonate with you and take ownership of them. This makes the journey more personal and the achievements truly yours.
- **Seeking Support on Your Terms:** It's alright to seek support, but ensure it's on your terms. Look for mentors who respect your autonomy and offer guidance without overstepping.

A Message to Guardians

To the guardians of these bright young individuals, remember that support doesn't mean steering. Offer your guidance and share your desires for them, but allow them the space to make these desires their own. Encourage their autonomy, celebrate their choices, and be there to support them through their successes and lessons learned.

When you understand that control and accountability are about finding a balance between pursuing desires and maintaining autonomy over one's life choices, you unlock the power to navigate your path with confidence, embrace challenges with resilience, and shape your destiny with a sense of purpose and self-direction. It's a delicate dance, but open communication, mutual respect, and a clear understanding of oneself can lead to a fulfilling and autonomous life.

In this section, Jon shares the concept of desire and its significance in the journey of young adults. His words serve as a guide, lighting the path for those navigating the complexities of growing up and finding their place in the world.

Here are quotes from Jon as he shares his wisdom and insights:

- **On the Nature of Desire:** "Desire is essentially about wanting something because we believe it will bring us happiness. It's a powerful force that can guide us toward our goals and dreams. But it's important to distinguish between desires that are truly our own and those influenced by others."
- **On Accountability and Control**: "Many young adults hesitate to pursue their desires because of the accountability and responsibility that come with them. They fear losing control. But accountability doesn't mean giving up freedom; it's about taking ownership of your path and your decisions."
- **On Seeking Help**: "Asking for help isn't a sign of weakness; it's a step towards understanding and fulfilling your desires. A coach or a mentor can offer guidance, not by dictating what you should do, but by illuminating possibilities and helping you navigate through them."
- **On Facing Fears**: "The fear of accountability often masks a deeper fear of failure. It's okay to be scared. Acknowledging and confronting this fear is the first step towards overcoming it. Remember, every successful person has faced and conquered their fears."
- **On Growth and Desire**: "True growth happens when we step out of our comfort zones. Your desires, even the ones that scare you, are growth opportunities. They push you to explore who you are and what you truly want from life."

- **On Making Decisions**: "When faced with a decision, especially one tied to a deep desire, ask yourself: Does this path align with who I am and want to be? Your inner voice is a powerful guide. Listen to it, trust it, and let it lead you."

- **On the Journey of Discovery**: "The pursuit of desires is more than just achieving goals. It's a journey of discovery, learning, and personal development. Embrace the journey with an open heart and mind. The experiences you gain are just as valuable as the outcomes."

- **On Empowerment through Desire**: "Harnessing your desires is about empowerment. It's about knowing what you want and going after it with conviction. Remember, your desires are a reflection of your deepest aspirations. Honor them, pursue them, and let them guide you to your fullest potential."

Through my words, I aim to inspire both young adults and their parents to view the concept of desire with curiosity, openness, and courage. My insights serve as a reminder that while the journey to fulfilling our desires is filled with challenges, it also presents abundant opportunities for growth, learning, and self-discovery.

Section 15
LEGACY AND LESSONS: JON'S REFLECTIONS

Hey everyone, it's Jon here. I'm coming to you with a heart full of stories, experiences, and insights I've gathered over the years. Today, I want to share with you the memories of my past and the lessons they've taught me. I hope they light your path a bit brighter.

The Digital Revolution: A Gateway to the World

Reflecting on the inventions that significantly impacted my life, the computer and the internet stand out. These marvels opened up a universe of knowledge and connection that was previously unimaginable. I remember talking to my son, Cody, via Skype while he was stationed in Afghanistan. The thought that we could see and speak to each other across such vast distances was nothing short of miraculous back then. It showcased the incredible power of technology to bring us closer to making the world a smaller, more connected place.

From Party Lines to Instant Communication

Growing up, the concept of a party-line phone system was our reality. Fast-forward to today, and the evolution of smartphones is astounding. This leap from shared lines to personal, instant communication devices underscores the incredible pace of technological advancement. It reminds us to appreciate the conveniences we often take for granted and to use these tools to foster genuine connections.

The Echoes of History: Lessons from the Past

In my lifetime, events like the assassinations of Martin Luther King Jr. and John F. Kennedy deeply affected me. These moments of national tragedy taught me about resilience, the power of a united community, and the importance of striving for justice and equality. Similarly, witnessing the first man walk on the moon was a testament to human ingenuity and the boundless potential of our collective endeavor. These historical milestones serve as powerful reminders of where we've come from and where we have the potential to go.

The Power of Sports and Determination

Athletics played a pivotal role in my life, teaching me about determination, teamwork, and the pursuit of excellence. Whether it was nearly pitching a no-hitter or playing Division One college football, sports instilled a mindset of perseverance and hard work. To the young ones out there, remember that this determination and focus can open doors you never thought possible. Embrace the challenges, for they are opportunities in disguise.

Embracing Change and Making It Fun

In talking with my grandkids and reflecting on my journey, what stands out is the importance of embracing change and finding joy in the journey. Life is indeed much gentler than the stories we tell about it. It's about making the most of the moments, finding joy in the small things, and not taking ourselves too seriously.

As I share these reflections, I hope they inspire you to look at your own life's journey with a sense of wonder and optimism.

Life is a mosaic of experiences, each piece colored by our choices, our challenges, and our joys. Embrace it all, learn from it, and remember, always find a reason to smile and laugh along the way.

Thank you for tuning in and sharing this journey with me. Remember, share the love, and spread the fun. Life's too precious not to enjoy it to the fullest. Until next time, take care and keep moving forward.

Feb 23, 2024

CONCLUSION BY JON ANFINSON

The term "wingman" originally comes from aviation, referring to a pilot who flies alongside and supports another pilot in a potentially dangerous mission, such as combat. In a broader social context, a wingman is someone who assists or supports another person, typically in a social or romantic setting. The role of a wingman can vary depending on the situation but often involves providing moral support, helping to initiate conversations, boosting confidence, or even deflecting attention from unwanted suitors. Essentially, a wingman is a trusted ally who has your back and enables you to navigate social interactions with greater ease and confidence.

Even though I have been Amy's and others' Wingman, I want you to know I hope to be yours as well. Imagine that.

Your Wing Man,

Jon

AFTERWARD BY AMY ANFINSON

Dear friends and family,

Jon passed peacefully on May 28, 2024, at 3:33 am. Though he never got to physically hold this book in his hands, I know that from the other realm, he will see it and be overjoyed that you now hold it in yours.

I remember sitting across from an intuitive in Sedona, Arizona, many years ago, who described Jon as a unique human with a heart of gold, salt of the earth. Fast-forward to today—writing The Wingman made sense. Early on, after receiving his coaching degree, he named himself "Global Father." All he ever really wanted was to share his wisdom with others in a loving, kind, fatherly way.

To me, Jon was not only my husband but also my yes-man and wingman. In his eyes, I could be, do, or have anything. His love and kindness toward me and my children were priceless. He was one of the richest men I have ever known. I am blessed to have been loved by him and to have loved him.

As I go through his questions and answers from interviews, I am moved beyond tears. Watching him navigate his journey has profoundly inspired me, and I know that whatever I do after his departure will be done with the certainty that he remains my wingman, urging me to be bold and unafraid.

I will allow myself the time to feel the longing for his physical presence and not resist it. But I also know he will stay in contact with me. An hour after he transitioned, I asked Alexa to play "peaceful music" and he managed to have it to play "Three Little Birds" by Kasey Musgrave.

I had never heard that version before, but it was perfect. He had always said to me when I was stressed, "I'm not worried about you," which was a meaningful message that helped me trust that I would find my way.

So, his first message from the other side was loud and clear. "Don't worry about a thing 'cause every little thing is going to be alright. aka I'm not worried about you." The message brings me peace that he is still with me and always will be in spirit.

As for us all, I know that a part of him will always live in our hearts, and those touched by him, whether in person or through this book, can fuel their soul purpose to continue his and their own legacy for the greater good.

So, as you hold this book and wonder about your next steps to align with your highest self, take it as a sign. Know that you now have a wingman who desires the very best for you.

Let me end by saying, "I'm not worried about you." Having studied what I call the Faith Frequency Formula, I trust that you have what it takes to make your life better.

So, *I'm not worried about you.*

All the best.

With love,
Amy
The better it gets, the better it gets.

ACKNOWLEDGEMENTS

First and foremost, I extend my heartfelt gratitude to my beloved wife, Amy, whose strength, love, and unwavering support have sustained me through the highs and lows of life. Your courage in the face of adversity continues to inspire me every day. Thank you for letting me be your Yes Man and Wing Man!

I am immensely thankful to my family for their unconditional love and unwavering belief in my dreams. Your encouragement has been a constant source of inspiration and motivation, and I am blessed to have you by my side.

I am beyond grateful and always inspired by all* of my kids and grandkids, who have given in so many ways. I am so proud of each and every one of you. I am blessed. *There is no such thing as a stepchild.

To my friends, family and mentors, thank you for your invaluable guidance, wisdom, and encouragement throughout this journey. I was in awe of how you showed up at all the right times. I deeply appreciate you all for never leaving our side during hard times. You are amazing friends. Your insights and support have been instrumental in shaping my life into what it is today. Your love and dedication have enriched me and all that I have touched.

I deeply thank everyone who helped care for me, drove me to and from appointments, and the care from Season's Hospice. A special thanks to Kandy for her live-in and loving care over the last three months and to my brother-in-law Ryan for helping make it happen.

As I reach the culmination of this journey, I am humbled and deeply grateful for the myriad of individuals who have contributed to the creation of this book, namely Judy Cochrane, writer, editor and owner of R House Publishing LLC and also LoriAnn Garner who compiled our sessions in Part Two. Their inspiration, support and unwavering belief in my legacy have been the driving force behind this endeavor. Thank you to Emma Elziga - who created the book cover and interior layout. The cover is perfect! Thank you for your contributions, questions, and interviews - they have touched my heart in ways words cannot express, and I am eternally thankful for this gift.

I am grateful to the readers who have embraced my words and allowed them to resonate in their hearts. Your support and encouragement fuel my passion for storytelling, and I am honored to have been able to share this journey with you.

Last but not least, I express my profound gratitude to God for the inspiration and love that guides me and all that have helped me on this path. Your presence is felt in every word, and I am forever grateful for the opportunity to channel your light into the world. See you soon.

With love and appreciation,
Your Wing Man,
Jon Anfinson

CONNECT

www.amyanfinson.com

COMING SOON:

2024
blameLESS

2025
The Faith Frequency

by Amy Anfinson
co-authored by Jon
Anfinson - my wingman

(This book came to me two weeks before Jon's diagnosis and the *Faith Frequency* Formula unfolded during our 11 month journey)

www.ingramcontent.com/pod-product-compliance
Lightning Source LLC
Chambersburg PA
CBHW070627050426
42450CB00011B/3137